I0575704

"The 180 Degrees of Motivation *sanctifies the blessed literary talents of savants and thinkers who lived near the curve—in New Orleans. This work is a brilliant collaboration of thought and essay, placing it well above the curve as a masterfully executed and supremely crafted literary masterpiece.*"

– Greg Ward, MD

The 180 Rule of Motivation & Etc.

Essays, Poetry, Letters to Wynton Marsalis and The New York Times, and a Stage Play

Ken Mask

Published by:
KMS
Durham, North Carolina

ISBN: 979-8-9992700-0-9

First Edition: June 2025
Second Edition: July 2025

10 9 8 7 6 5 4 3 2

Distributed by:
Ingram Content Group
www.ingramcontent.com

Take service with such of its officers as
are worthy,
Make friends with such of its knights as
are Good.

Confucius

Between the acres of the rye

    These pretty countryfolk would lie.

    James Joyce, *Ulysses*

THE 180 RULE

Be, Become, and Go Beyond

CHAPTER ONE

Daunting tasks face us every day. Whether it is making a bed, sweeping floors, cleaning, clearing porches, doing the dishes, working out. A conversation a few moments ago with my magnificent cousin, Shaun Young, put me in the mood of discussing something I've employed in my life and with my kids entitled the "180 Rule."

Specifically, this is for children who do not immediately see the benefits of doing the chores, on any level at any time and well for that matter, this applies to anyone.

No one relishes a stack of dishes sitting in the sink, a few pots and pans on the stove, dishes all over the house, plates, glasses, etc.

In an effort to meditate during moments of duty, I've employed the 180 second rule. This entails taking a few long deep breathes and approaching a task at hand with reverence. Now, silently counting down, 180, 179, 178, 177, and during those moments of silent repose, you roll up your sleeves, take another deep breath, and then get to the task. For instance, with a stack of dishes; maybe been there for a full day or two.

This is cha cha do: merely pick up one plate, get some water going, get that good blue grey Brillo pad or that steel wool scrubber and begin. Clean that one plate, another, a bowl, another, a fork, spoon, get a glass, you go around the rim, tackle that metal, you put them to the side. These motions can be prep if you have a dishwasher or prep if you're going to use a rack. Now a pot or two, you put in some water to attack that baked on spaghetti sauce at the bottom..... dissolved a bit. Breath. Next you grab another plate, and meditatively continue the countdown 150, 149, 148..... three more glasses, scrub them, rinse them, put them to the side. If you have a dishwasher, you start loading that. If you don't, you get that big bucket of water that you can put these items in to run them, spread out a towel on the countertop nice and neatly spread out to use as a drying pad. Get the hot water running again, grab a few more dishes, scrub them, scrub them, squirt, squirt, scrub them, wipe, wipe, 120, 119, 118.

Now get to those pots that you have "soaking" and you get the favorite Brillo pad, go around it three or four times in a row. Make it a game. Go around and around a merry-go round, yada, yada, yada. Grab that other pot, get to it; and reach for yet other pot across the sink and the one on the stove and do the same thing. Those grits are mighty stiff by now, will need to scrub extra with elbow grease for those, but no problem and of course the water is flowing; 100, 99, 98.

Okay, getting the dishes done, on the way to being finished with a deep breathing meditation. Scan around the house; gather a few additional glasses/saucers that are on the nightstand, the coffee table, on the front porch and come back, 86, 85, 84, 83. Run water in them, splash, splash, splash, splash, rub, rub, rub. Those few are underway—soaking buckle, in the dishwasher. Oh, wait a minute; there are more items are still there; on the kitchen nook table. Okay. 70, 69, 68, 67.

Now load the dishwasher or use that bucket to put all the dishes in…. run hot water to rinse; smooth and spread that drying towel out; stack neatly on 'leans' to dry.

Take another deep breath…smile; task is almost done. You have 30 seconds left, 29, 28, 27. Wait a minute now. You forgot a few dishes in the oven! You get those; squirt, squirt, splash, splash, rub, rub, rub, Brillo pad, Brillo pad. You place them in the dishwasher. You look around. What else? Okay, there's the Lysol. Boom.

Next the 'finish up kitchen' task will be cake- the counters, spray them down, squirt, squirt, squirt, squirt, squirt. Get that clean towel out of the dish rack, wipe, wipe, wipe, wipe, 10, 9, 8, 7.

Lysol, squirt, squirt, squirt, wipe, wipe, wipe. The refrigerator door, squirt, squirt, squirt, wipe, wipe, wipe, 4, 3, 2, 1. Job well done. Job done. And it has been 180 seconds. Literally.

During this time of 'coming to zero,' you have in addition to completing a task that was DAUNTING, three minutes ago, allowed your subconscious to get to work. With this level of accomplishment and deep breathing, the conscious mind, busy with a chore and counting has freed up a dream state, so to speak, to work on that book/ novel you've been trying to start!

Again, as agreed most tasks are daunting. Most tasks in thought are bigger than the tasks themselves. Anything you need to get done, washing the dishes, getting the clothes 'ready' to wash , I used quotes, because you are not washing them; the machine is! Hehehehehe.

Okay. Let's say the car needs a little bit of dust busting and, oh, by the way, the backseat floor is full of McDonald's bags, cups, plates, all kinds of discarded mail, etc. Breath, breath; head out of the house, reach the hose. Breath, breath, start 180, 179, 178. Turn the hose on, spray, spray, spray. Oh, wait a minute, going to need some soap and water, go back into the house, get a bucket, squirt, squirt, a little dish-washing liquid, take it outside, spray water, 160, 159, 158. Take a rag, that is the good rag for washing cars, lather it up, spread it out, go to the hood, go to the top of the car, like we were taught, top to bottom, top to bottom, not bottom to top, top to bottom. Breath, count, 130, 129, 128 wipe, squirt more water, squirt, squirt, wash, wash, wash, wash, wash, wash, wash the sides, you get the sides, you walk around, you go to the sides, you hit the top again with the clean rag on the side of the little stair over there. Grab the hose, 100, 99, 98, spray, spray, spray clean, spray clean, 70, 69, 68.

Oh, wait a minute now, we have the trash in the back floor. Open the door, get a trash bag, which you keep handily in the door handle space. Take those items, 40, 39, 38, 37, 36; rounded trash, take a step back, you take a look at the car, look up, look down.

Get a towel out of the trunk and start to dry it, dry the top, wipe, wipe, wipe, dry the back, trunk, hood, side, side, side, side, side, side, 10, 9, 8, 7, 6, 5. You are done. With 5 seconds left. Whew. Take a deep breath. Take a breath of a job well done. A job done in 180 seconds.

By counting out down to 0, a state of freedom is secured. Zero is a very comfortable state of existence, mentally and physically. It is a place to relax and breathe and do things that are important. Zero is a subconscious level of divine engagement. It is the beginning of your life, times 0. It is the most comfortable time of existence.

There are millions of bits of information that flood into our subconsciousness every second. The conscious mind is able to process about 40 items per second and the remaining are missed out, simply not acknowledged or identified. One of the functions of a 'countdown' method is a state of meditative engagement. By counting down during a task, it allows the subconscious to engage with the bits of information that are coming away. It is like a dream state. When you are asleep at night and you are dreaming, your conscious mind is freed from its responsibility. Your subconscious takes over and that is when your true beliefs, desires, and resolutions come to light.

With the 180 rule, active engagement of meditative countdown frees you to solve other problems while you are doing the tasks, movement beyond doing your chore. This freedom delivers you subconscious the tool to dream and solve resolve other issues, concerns.

A popular management technique in business is the activity of timeboxing. To timebox is a use a select amount of energy for a certain period of time. Well, the 180 rule is a mini timebox. One is able to distill during this time period, not only a task to be done and completed, but also an exercise in subconscious delivery. In order to solve a problem; that is come up with 'a' solution to an issue, to perhaps clear a thought or engage an activity, an amount of freedom to relax and distance yourself from the task at hand and to contemplate an outcome is vital.

What happens with the 180 rule is that you give in. Giving in to intention and shifting attention to a subconscious state is powerful. The freedom received from getting the task done rather than having it "as" a task that needs to be done, is a channel of freedom from the subconscious. The subconscious mind allows a capacity for divine engagement. It is no longer a conscious activity, rather, it is a subconscious engagement, one is able to embrace a conflict, resolve a so-called conflict, and move beyond. The calm collective state permits one to go beyond. Going beyond a task is the most magnificent feeling in the world. You are able to check off a box. That in and of itself, in addition to getting the task done as a necessary component of chores, activities, engagements, and allows one to subconsciously move forward into a creative realm.

CHAPTER TWO

My examples—doing the dishes and washing the car—are just templates. You can apply the 180 Rule to any activity that feels like a chore or task, something unpleasant, or even something you know is good for you but still struggle to start.

Take working out, for instance. Obviously, a workout should last longer than 180 seconds on any level or intensity, but the *template* still works.

Let's say you have the thought: *I need to work out.* Then comes the hesitation—you start complaining or wondering whether you have your workout clothes, your gym gear, or your tennis shoes nearby. That's when you use the 180 Rule.

You look around. Maybe you don't see your favorite sweats right away, so you head into the next room—there they are. You're at 170. Then you find your favorite T-shirt and socks—160, 159, 158, 157.

Next, you go to the kitchen, look behind the door, and there are your tennis shoes. You put them on. Now, use the next 120 seconds to stretch. Take deep breaths. Move your limbs. Swing your arms.

50, 49, 48, 47...

Then you head to your workout space—maybe it's your apartment balcony, your front porch, the backyard, or maybe you hop on your bike or into your car.

10, 9, 8...

That's the 180 Rule applied to *getting ready* to work out. Something you *know* you need to do. Once you get to your workout location, you can apply the 180 Rule again.

Push-ups. Sit-ups. Squats. Jumping jacks. Stretches.

Start the countdown: 180, 179, 178...

Stretch. Reach for your toes. Reach for the sky. Stretch to the side. Twist your shoulders. Twist your back.

150, 149...

Break each individual exercise into a mini 180-second burst and get it done.

See? It fits almost anywhere.

Illustrations, examples... yada, yada, yada.

CHAPTER THREE

The resistance to a task is often more striking than the task itself. But with the right focus and mindset, anything is possible.

So, you want to write that book, right? Want to tell your story?

The same principle applies. How about using good old-fashioned pen and paper—or pencil and paper? They're probably lying around somewhere. Huh. Grab a notepad. Write down, from the beginning of your life to now, whatever you feel like sharing. Make it bullet points if that helps. Okay—breathe, and start:

180, 179, 178...

"I grew up in this small town—or this city, or this state—and I experienced this, and that, and the other..."

150, 149...

By the time you've counted down to 1, you've started your book.

End of story.

What's happening subconsciously when you engage in a task this way—when you move with this level of intention and focus—is that you're actually healing. Not just yourself, but your past. And, in a sense, the past of those around you.

This isn't just about "setting an example." It's deeper than that. You are aligning your spirit and vibrations in a way that begins to correct past failures and opens you to future possibility.

By placing the 180 Rule into your consciousness, you align your spiritual fortitude. Paradoxically, the 180 Rule—as a geometric reference—represents a complete reversal. Of course, 360 degrees brings you full circle, returning to where you started. But 180 takes you in a completely different direction.

And that direction can vary depending on your alignment. If your inner compass is off, you may need to return to 180 degrees of thought and reflection to realign. When you do, it helps not only with the task at hand, but with your greater personal path—your arrangement and your trajectory.

That trajectory, once realigned, becomes perfectly attuned—not just to your own rhythm, but to those around you and to the greater, complicated universe, often without you even realizing it.

Subconsciously, you reach into a state of clarity, of calm—a kind of nirvana—that opens a pathway to all kinds of recovery. If things are going spectacularly well in your life, the 180 Rule deepens that momentum. If things are not going well, it helps you reset.

The 180 Rule allows you to set a course.

Pause… Just for a moment.

Put this text down. Step away from your phone, your tablet—whatever is pulling at your attention.

Now, as part of practicing *The 180 Rule*, I challenge you: take a breath, clear your mind, and count slowly from 180 to 0. Then do it again. And again if you need to.

This simple act is more than a countdown—it's a reset. A mental and spiritual recalibration that brings clarity and direction.

Whenever anxiety creeps in—or even when life feels amazing—take a moment to be fully present. Feel the wonder of being alive on this spinning globe, moving boldly through the universe.

The 180 Rule isn't just an exercise. It's a mindset. A reminder that no matter where you start, forward is always an option. Progress is always possible. And purpose is always within reach.

& Etc.

*Essays, Poetry, Letters to Wynton Marsalis
and The New York Times, and a Stage Play*

New Orleans, Old and New

The thing that struck anyone who knew or had heard about New Orleans was the 'old' feeling that permeated the space. The city had been settled early in our nation's history and boasted some of the most distinguished landmarks and individuals who had called the place home.

The birthplace of jazz, a destination for great food, a keeper of the flame of early- and late-night 'good times,' and warm hospitality—the area on the curve of the Mississippi River, termed the Crescent City, was unique and remained so. No other city in the history of mankind had experienced the displacement of an entire populace. Not to make light of the extreme destruction of property, the loss of life, and the altered psyche of all who experienced the flooding as a result of Hurricane Katrina—I merely wanted to champion the call for hope. New Orleans stood out in an outstanding way. The events of the week of August 29, 2005, were a wake-up call for us to treat one another with respect. Rushing floodwaters, pounding people, places, and spaces—changing land, mind, and roots—presented unprecedented trauma.

I had lived and worked in New Orleans for the past ten years. Other cities I had called home could not compare: the climate was excellent year-round; the landscape was a marvelous mixture of evergreen grass, oaks, ferns, and bright red dogwoods; the bayous, ponds, and lakes were delightful; the airport was twenty minutes from the farthest point; the French Quarter likely held some record for having the most densely packed collection of establishments dedicated to a good time; the buildings in all sections (wards) were wonderful examples of architecture from around the world; and the people living and working there were the type of folk you met and instantly considered friends and family. That might have sounded corny and trite, but after being asked by so many people over the past three months—What do you think about New Orleans? Will they rebuild it? Will it be the same? Will people you know come back to live? Will they fix the levees? And so on—I had to say it.

I realized then, sitting in an airplane seat at roughly 33,000 feet above the ground, that those and other sorts of questions were, in many ways, silly and shortsighted. Having just browsed the *New York Times* Sunday edition from December 4, 2005—which covered world topics ranging from the war to a book review on Samuel Johnson's *Dictionary: Defining the World*—I felt compelled to add my opinion to the matter of rebuilding a city.

Diane Raines Ward's book, *Water Wars*, was a fine example of an "I told you so" type of work. In it, she superbly covered the history of flooding, dams, levees, water needs, rivers, lakes, and political musings. The book read like a novel while discussing topics one usually encountered in environmental studies textbooks or earth science classes. Moreover, I had just finished Kurt Vonnegut's *A Man Without a Country*, which was a brilliant collection of his thoughts about the universe. His humor was best summarized in: "What is life all about? We are here to help each other get through this thing, whatever it is." These two thinkers had set the stage for me to delve into this essay.

New Orleans would be fine. We would have it back in a few years—after folks had moved past the trauma and horror brought about by both nature and human error. Period. The suffering would continue, and the anguish that came from the loss of lives and property would stay in our minds forever.

There were groups of people using the best of their abilities to come together in the effort to rebuild this city. I saw, from the vantage point of having lived there, having visited as a child growing up in North Carolina, and being sent to vacation with my mother's relatives, that the warmth and determined energy of all inhabitants and journeymen/women who had enjoyed the space—and the teams of thinkers coming together to restore the city—would ensure that things were up and running soon. All was not well in Smallsville. The mighty Casey had struck out, but other pitches were coming.

That brought me to the topic at hand from a technological standpoint. The fact that I could write and edit those thoughts on a piece of metal and plastic machinery, viewing the words on a lit screen while traveling in another piece of machinery at 33,000 feet—to traverse a distance that would have taken months to cover less than 100 years ago—spoke to my confidence in the matter. I didn't continue with such banal phrases as, "If we can put a man on the moon…" or "We live in an age of…" Rather, I said the Crescent City would soon enjoy the flavorful vitality we all knew and loved.

I personally knew people there—like Matt Dillon, Elmo and Mike Dix, Lincoln Alexis, Mike Dunbar, Glenn and Morris Wilson, John Calcote, and Karl Washington—who were literally rebuilding, gutting, and replacing damaged materials in homes and businesses throughout the city. And a man like Wynton Marsalis, who had a table the size of what one would imagine the Pentagon used to outline war, which hosted a strategic map-type model of New Orleans as he assisted in city planning and rebuilding.

It was with sober research, analysis, insight, strategy, and energy that we would have Old New Orleans back to enjoy.

Ballet Against Deadly Forces

Bullfighting. Sport? Art?
Cultural phenomenon? Fashion statement?

Death in the Afternoon has long been a favorite for anyone seeking a substantive review and description of bullfighting. Hemingway's book offers a poignant and penetrating examination of the activity from multiple perspectives: the nobility and honor of the matadors who risk their lives in the arena, discussions on cruelty to animals, the pageantry of the sport, what makes a great matador, the bloodlines that produce the best bulls, and general reflections on the art—from both inside the ring and behind the scenes. He also addresses the cultural importance of bullfighting worldwide... and the "suits of light" that the men—and now women—wear, which are nothing short of dazzling.

Bullfighting has long been considered controversial due to the suffering that participating animals endure—at the hands (horns) of the bulls, and at the hands (blades) of the picadors, matadors, and ring assistants. The horses on which picadors ride often bear the brunt of the bull's fury, and the bulls themselves suffer obvious insult and injury. The pros and cons will continue to be debated, but not here. As Hemingway said, there are those who enjoy the sport and those who do not, for a number of reasons. Just as there is a portion of the population that rejects prizefighting and calls for its abolition, animal rights activists lobby for the end of bullfighting.

The stance here is simply to report on the pageantry of the art form and to review some thoughts from one of its leading figures: El Juli.

Research for this discussion included articles from the Internet—primarily from bullfights.org and various matadors' websites. The project was originally inspired by an introductory article published years ago in a European magazine, which profiled "El Juli," Julian Lopez Escobar, the then-new wunderkind—a "shot of energy" for the bullfighting world. At the time, he was 18 years old and had taken the sport by storm, demonstrating a natural disposition for style and grace. He began working in Mexico at age 16, since Spanish regulations do not allow matadors to perform until they are 18. Within two years, he rose to the top of the profession and now enjoys the kind of recognition and endorsement deals Michael Jordan received during his peak.

Talent and hard work pay off. The occasion presented itself: Spain's El Juli was scheduled to perform within "striking distance" of New Orleans, in Mexicali, Mexico. The venue was the new Gran Corrida de Lujo, located just off Independence Avenue, on Sunday, January 30, 2005. The playbill also included two celebrated Mexican participants: Rafael Ortega and Fernando Ochoa.

Bullfighting events are staged year-round around the globe. The "season" is a literal traveling enterprise: Spain, Portugal, France, Mexico, Venezuela.

We arrived in Mexicali on Friday afternoon, January 28, 2005—two days before the match. In-house counsel John K. Miller and I checked into the Crowne Plaza Hotel, a local five-star establishment just ten minutes from the American-Mexican border. The hotel had the elegant, old-world charm of a place that sincerely welcomes guests—not with flashy gestures, but with genuine kindness and the understanding that guests are special and deserving of care. Manager Carlos and bellhops Juan, Luis, and others greeted us with warmth and grace.

Our first day included casual meetings with hotel staff and local fans gathered in the lobby, where the excitement for the upcoming bullfight was palpable. We were fortunate to meet and quickly befriend a few American aficionados of the sport: Dean and Tina Reineman, and photographer Luis Arellano. We interviewed them formally—with the tape recorder rolling—and later in more casual settings while enjoying the sights of the arena. The conversations were natural, the kind that form when people recognize a shared passion—the spark of true friendship.

Our first meal in the town was at La Vasquez on Heroes Street, a charming restaurant offering old-school, service-oriented hospitality. The menu featured grilled Cornish hen, vegetable soup, and freshly prepared guacamole. Dinner the next day at Laguna Azul included a cold, ceviche-like seafood cocktail served in large glass bowls: shrimp, octopus, oysters, squid, and freshly steamed fish, all dressed in lemon juice and spicy salsa. At both places, the beer was ice-cold, and the margaritas were "righteous."

That day:

Early morning ceremonies led to the afternoon bullfights, beginning with the sortie, where bulls were presented and assigned via lottery. With permission, members of the media, aficionados, managers, breeders, and handlers gathered in the backstage corrals to observe the herd. Matadors solemnly picked numbers from a hat to determine which bulls they would face, each forming a cross with the ticket over chest and forehead before kissing the crumpled slip. It was a sacred moment. Each sought a brave bull—not one so wild and unpredictable as to pose uncontrollable danger.

Later, around noon, came the pre-event ritual, where the matadors gathered to don their *traje de luces* (suit of lights), pray, and share moments of camaraderie. The tension built steadily. All appeared appropriately nervous yet undeniably brave. At the sound of the opening bell, in parade-like fashion, the matadors, banderilleros, picadors, and support staff marched into the arena.

By that point, crowds outside had already been entertained with flamenco dances, mariachi bands, vendors offering local fare, and tailgating festivities. The atmosphere buzzed with anticipation as old friends reunited and new ones connected. Spectators took their seats—sun or shade—and prepared for the show, where each of the three matadors would face two bulls, alternating turns.

Primary excitement centered on three elements: (1) the bull's reaction to its first exposure to humans—having been raised on isolated ranches to preserve its wild instinct; (2) the matador's ability to engage the animal with honor and skill; and (3) the overall grace, elegance, and respect demonstrated toward the beast.

The crowd served as a vocal collective judge—responding with cheers, whistles, jeers, or handkerchief-waving to the matador's bravery, style, and finesse. However, the final judgment lay with three official judges, seated in a prime viewing box, who assessed performances and awarded trophies based on criteria only years of experience could explain.

Later that evening, El Juli joined us at the hotel sports bar to celebrate the day's success. He was gracious and engaging, immediately noticing the copy of *Death in the Afternoon* on our table. A translator assisted during the conversation, and he warmly expressed his gratitude for the opportunity to talk with us and answer our questions.

Interview Excerpt:

Who do you read?: "Hugo and Cervantes."

Where do you see yourself in twenty years?: "Teaching. Breeding."

How do you relax before a match?: "Resting in my room. Praying."

Do you have a favorite suit of lights?: "No. I went through sixty last year."

What American art forms do you follow?: "Jazz music. Baseball."

How do you assess the bull's temperament?: "I take it as it comes—judge the demeanor with each pass."

Are you afraid?: "I am cautious."

How do you view your place in the history of the sport?: "I don't. I am just doing a job."

The one question I wish I'd asked: "Which hand is your dominant one?"

I've never seen a discussion about whether a matador being left- or right-handed affects performance—though it seems likely, given the difficult techniques involved. Perhaps I'll have to attend another afternoon match and find out.

Afterward, El Juli continued a game of pool—banking the eight ball into the corner pocket with ease and a bright smile. That kind of relaxed effortlessness is the stuff of greatness. We were grateful for the time we spent with him during his visit.

Look for Julián López Escobar to do even greater things in and out of the arena. He was respectful, well-mannered, and gracious—retiring from the gathering early to rest for the upcoming season.

El Juli

It is always a pleasant experience to be introduced to a new acquaintance—especially when that person greets you with a warm hug that includes a firm grasp of your opposite arm and a shoulder nestled in the center of your chest, with heads gently touching at the ears during the embrace. Such was my first interaction with one of the world's greatest matadors.

Bullfighting is a cultural event celebrated across the globe. As previously mentioned, Hemingway did a fantastic job both discussing and romanticizing the sport/art in his 1930s work, which has since become a classic introduction to the world of bullfighting. His writing serves as a thoroughly articulated document that addresses nearly every angle from which the tradition can be viewed. Research into this cultural phenomenon is essential for anyone seeking to better understand the close-knit world of matadors—their training, education, the bulls themselves, and the people who support the *corrida de lujo*.

Just as many great athletes are reluctant to give interviews prior to a major event, so too are the world's premier matadors often hesitant to discuss their art form in the days or hours leading up to a match. This may stem from a combination of superstition, busy schedules, and nerves. Nevertheless, we were fortunate enough to cross paths with El Juli on the evening before an event in Mexicali, Mexico—January 29, 2004. He arrived with his small entourage late that Saturday evening at the Crowne Plaza Hotel.

Thanks to the quick friendships we formed with two hotel staff members—concierge Carlos Marquez and bellhop Luis—the meeting and interview were made possible. Carlos had informed hotel management of our request, and Luis graciously served as our translator. We met in the hotel's cozy sports bar, just off the lobby, seated at a round, card-table-style booth. We were served a superior pot of coffee—undoubtedly the beverage of choice for someone preparing for a high-stakes match, avoiding the mind-altering effects of alcohol to keep a clear and focused mind.

The introduction was comfortable, and we soon dove into a series of predetermined questions.

Easing into a discussion of his personal journey into the sport, we quickly established a strong rapport and mutual respect. Our conversation revealed his thoughtful reflections on the place he had carved out for himself in the storied world of bullfighting.

Dear Wynton

Dear Wynton:

As you know, one of the great things about traveling is the opportunity to meet people like Granny Grump and her close-knit family in El Centro, California.

I stopped by Sally's Book Nook, located at 235 Main Street, this past weekend on my way to Mexicali for the bullfights with John Kennedy Miller, and had the chance to visit the quaint establishment on Saturday afternoon. The town, situated in Southernmost California—about two hours southeast of San Diego and just fifteen minutes from the Mexican border—sits along a Main Street that runs right through the heart of things.

Their family-run place has been there for 23 years, upholding a tradition of warm, friendly watering holes and coffee spots where you can enjoy a superior cup of fresh brew and meet folks with the sincerity of people who aren't afraid to be kind.

The cozy, homey, well-lit shop has two distinct sides that reflect the gentle art of doing things with humility. One side caters to school supply needs and readers looking for everything from novels and cookbooks to history books, GED study guides, and graduate education materials. The other side features a small Danish/snack counter alongside a gourmet coffee shop. Scattered around the room are turn-of-the-century photos depicting California's early development. Dinette-style tables provide a welcoming space to enjoy a bite to eat and actually talk—really talk—about your thoughts on any subject.

I'm grateful for such interactions.

Ken

Letter to the Editor:
The New York Times Book Review

At this point, I am at the zenith of my disgust with the trite manner in which books are reviewed in your publication. Writers who fit a neat, charming pattern of "topics for discussion" are given preferential, witty, solid, glowing, and favorable reviews. Those like Stanley Crouch—whose work *The Artificial White Man* was discussed by Emily Eakin in "Battling Gangsters and Hussies" (January 16, 2005 issue)— are not afforded the same careful, unbiased critique.

Her piece reflects the kind of narrow-minded, obviously unedited, and clearly unfinished *drivel* that too often goes to print. Much of the review amounts to little more than attacks on isolated passages from the book, with roughly one-fifth of the article consisting of quoted excerpts—one of which Eakin responds to with a juvenile: "Huh?" This single-word reaction illustrates the level of her banal sophistication and lack of understanding.

Crouch's prose is precise and brilliant. It is nowhere near "sloppy... nor crude."

His ability to cover a wide range of topics with grace, ease, and elegance—on what he calls his "civilizing mission," combating the coarseness, vacuity, crude stereotypes, and ethnic groupthink of American culture—demonstrates his genius.

Someone has to do it.

What Eakin demonstrates, by contrast, is the ability to scan material, regurgitate clichés from "book review" manuals, and perpetuate the very elementary mentation that Crouch, like a noble matador, seeks to slay.

Fashion for the Home

The *body* can be draped in clothing to suit the occasion—to stay cool, to stand out, or to "fly to the moon" with that certain someone. When we go to the mall or a boutique, we're often looking for items that will help us make a statement, stay on-trend, and feel confident. Most people know which colors look good on them, what styles fit their vibe, and what kind of gear is appropriate for an afternoon hangout, a festive gathering, or an evening on the town.

But this same element of style often doesn't translate to the *places* we live. When outfitting our living spaces, we tend to focus on the essentials: the right appliances, a decent TV, coffee tables, bedroom sets, dinnerware, and drapes. The one thing we often overlook—the element that truly sets an abode apart—is the right *art*.

A person's *home* deserves the same attention we usually give to our wardrobes. Look around your space and ask yourself: How can I set—or rather, reset—these rooms apart? To make the leap from simply comfortable and functional to styled and sophisticated, a single, special piece of *art* can make all the difference.

There are a few brilliant artists in and around the New Orleans area who can effortlessly elevate your "cool meter." First to come to mind:

- J. Renee, a Xavier graduate, brings vibrant colors of the tropics, the lush warmth of the South, and Afro-Caribbean–inspired hues into stunning abstract expressions.

- Lionel Milton has an exquisite eye for flavored realism. His pieces pulse with motion and excitement, speaking directly to the energy of life.

- Los Angeles artist Emmy Lu, a frequent presence in the New Orleans art scene, adds textured depictions of families, homes, and churches—the places we hold dear—bringing a deep sense of home, even if you're already there.

Contact any of these creative geniuses for a piece of art—and history—for your home.

A Cape Code Vacation

The northeastern U.S. region known as Cape Cod is the kind of unique getaway that can best be described with a carefully chosen collection of words—ideally by someone with the linguistic command reserved for a few piercingly discriminating thinkers. The ability of this correspondent to capture the essence of the place and translate the deep well of impressions into a body of material that does the area justice is, admittedly, suboptimal... and thus, I pause.

But wait. I'll try.

The winding two-lane highway leading into Cape Cod is beautifully announced by a large, carefully manicured brush-and-scrub cutout—one that speaks volumes about the region's dedication to rest and relaxation. Yet, the area does not exhibit the kind of anxious need to impress found in many traditional "summer destinations." Instead, the landscape is a harmonious blend of lush green foliage and light-tan, sandy dunes—soft, beach-hilled plains where land and ocean meet in a cove seemingly created to remind us that there is, indeed, a God... and that He or She wants you to take a moment and let your body rest.

The long stretch of Route 6 carries the vacationer some 40 miles through towns whose names honor Native American villages—names that should grace signs across all of the United States. At the end of that road lies Provincetown, often regarded as the true terminus of the Cape. There, visitors encounter a centrally located stone ledger and a towering monument that pierces the foggy mists of dawn and dusk, proudly commemorating the first settlers who landed on these rocky shores before continuing on to Plymouth Rock—as every resident will gladly remind you.

"P-town" has a rare way of allowing individuals to simply *be*—to exist without the burden of social constraint, as reflected in its open and expressive culture. Enough said.

The scenery here is the kind you see on postcards—but in person, it's even more remarkable. With the naked eye, you can tell: there's no airbrushing. It's simply, and stunningly, real.

Louis: A Silent Film That Speaks Volumes

Typically, we enjoy a movie when the house lights go down and the screen lights up, accompanied by a recorded score. On recent occasions, however, attorney and musician Dan Pritzker's silent film *Louis* has toured the West Coast in a much more immersive and artistic fashion. This collaborative "art from the heart" allows audiences to experience the texture of brilliant storytelling, cinematography, and character development in splendid form.

In this unique presentation, the musical score is performed live from the orchestra pit by a band led by the incomparable Wynton Marsalis, featuring Cecile Licad, Carlos Henriquez, and Jason Marsalis.

During a post-performance interview with the legendary John Clayton, Wynton shared that Pritzker played a major role in selecting the music for the entire movie. With pride— and a hint of humor—he said that Dan knew *his* music better than most, diving deep into selections and getting his hands "short-of-ink-dirty," while Wynton composed the main theme and stylishly arranged personal tunes to add flavor to the film. With musicians from his standard ensemble, Jazz at Lincoln Center Orchestra (including Carlos Henriquez), as well as international talent, the result is nothing short of superb.

I recently had the pleasure of seeing *Louis* in Port Townsend, Washington. The bustling crowd arrived with great eagerness at the Centrum, a beautifully preserved 100-year-old airport hangar nestled in the hills of the quaint town. This was followed by a performance at Seattle's glorious Paramount Theatre—the kind of place where you can enjoy a truly elegant evening. *Louis* is, without question, the kind of film experience you'll want to see again and again.

The movie delivers a refreshing dynamic interplay on many levels. The opening scenes—set in 1907 New Orleans—are richly layered, with French Quarter establishments that pull you into the period through stunning direction and design. With a silent film, the actors must *show* every emotion, and the filmmakers must *capture* each moment—and *Louis* accomplishes this in Olympian form.

Actor, producer, and director Lucky Johnson recently remarked during a play rehearsal that he likes the word "action" as a derivative of "actor." He emphasized that the *movement* of an actor often carries a story more powerfully than words. In today's film world, we're accustomed to dialogue driving the narrative through set-up, first act, second act, and so on toward resolution. But in *Louis*, we follow the action of the actors—thanks to expert direction, outstanding performances, and carefully orchestrated scenes.

The film is a beautiful blend of drama, comedy, and music that propels the story forward. This period piece follows a young Louis Armstrong as he navigates the world of hardship and craft, fueled by unbridled enthusiasm, on the heroic trajectory toward becoming one of our nation's most iconic musical figures. The actors deliver textured, nuanced performances that make the story easy to follow with energy and authenticity. A brief scene featuring jazz legend Buddy Bolden—portrayed by Anthony Mackie—speaks volumes to the power of silent film to convey emotion and intensity.

Dr. Pritzker and his chosen team have done a magnificent job. He could not have selected a more fitting collaborative partner than Mr. Marsalis to bring this vision to life.

Score: Five Trumpets

Keeping

Water, as it travels over vast plains of life,
like calm bayou streams, roaring oceans, and iced-over lake
surfaces, flowing forth
with no anxiety,
keeps changing.

Water is:
- wave,
- still,
- breaking,
- retreating.

It works over rocks
and stones with the patience of Job,
Changing that which is
and that which has been
making that which will be.

So too, I keep this motion,
making my way over your vastness,
crashing against your shores,
and splashing onto your rocky past.

Pounding and carving my form
in you and sharing my desires
for our future.

Testing and Waiting

The stroke of midnight lands fast on my doorstep.

It is that 'right' of night;

This hammer-strike-posted reminder that there is yet more

darkness ahead

speaks to the world of fixed emotions.

Please take notice

and embrace your desires with this steadfast million,

blue-black darkness.

Slice these moments in your heart

and serve your soul.

Wait, shhhhhhhh.

It is dawn.

It is a new day,

and it is time for her breath:

tasting, ahead of her whisper

you are taught,

you capture her voice for all eternity,

satisfied.

Waiting

Patiently, moments pass with their own haste,
never changing their meter,
never altering their purpose.

This is the way it has been,
and this is the way it will be.

Yet, I have something quite different in mind for time.

Traveling at the speed of thought, to awaken eons past
and champion forth an era ahead,
like distant star-lit skies
and vast depths of existence yet realized,
I make this reality.
I am the future,
and all that is there belongs to me.
I have no purpose,
and no reason to waste time with time.

Snow Capped Plains on the Trail of the Life

Snowcapped plains on the trail of life are my route.

I skate over icy ponds in the heart of winter,
I seek your voice
in my daydreams
and flow forward.

Resting on a torn trunk,
once giant in the annals of time.

The true magnitude of this moment
becomes a reality.

Taking my gear
and proceeding over these snowcapped plains of life,
I move toward you and your heart.

A light, which is a beacon
for one chord,
to be played,
and a heart to be kindled,
awaits.

Purpose

Oh, that this torn page
will serve a better purpose now.

If I may make a point
having met you,

I say 'hello' here with this ink.
Needing nothing more,
I am quite fulfilled.

This torn piece of paper lets me
Speak, it lets me scream.

Having met you and needing to
Express it, I am quite done.

Sweet Rapture

Thoughts of you keep me warm
and comfortable.

Speaking with you keeps me calm
and safe.

Because,
When a kind and wonderful angel
makes its appearance on Earth
and when opportunity comes from across
time and space,
this is a blessing.

When a spirit with depth and sensibility
walks through one's gate,
take notice and enjoy the good fortune
and walk gently with humility and soulfulness, onward.

Creek Side

The creek carries
all times past.

Floating onward and
over pebbles, rocks and branches,
the creek's spirit carries
eons of thought.

The creek flows within
its own path with swiftness, confidence
and calmly the delivers
its soul and purpose
with no fear.

The creek moves
with grace
and style
over objects and things.

And, if you are lucky to stand
and to stare 'creek side,'
let your flowing spirit
be carried away
into the eons of time.

Trane Thoughts

I don't have much hear to say.

Words escape my net, they are lost in your ocean,
yet still this
flood of ideas
seeks release.

How do I discover within
my heart the true essence
of my existence?

Malachi,
Coltrane:
that's it.

I have but one source of true words
and he is wondrous;
I feel his warmth and humility throughout.

This set of ideas rushed forward
as I blindly set about this task
and now I must resolve my own thoughts as a human.

To You

I will suck dry the oceans and seas before I let this fire
within me,
that burns like none other,
be extinguished.

The crust of each cavern, each chiasm
will be like a dust bowl,
and parched creatures will scream
for life
before I leave this task undone.

To reach you, by walking
on an ocean's bottom.

Dunne

Don't deny me you.

Just as light from a distant star burns
and arrives within our sphere with its brilliance,
long after its time and its flames have died
out,
your charm,
wisdom,
and grace
have traveled this way.

Patiently,
I await your arrival.

Patiently
your brilliance will be captured.

Silent now!

I am waiting.

Sweet Serenity

Stars borrow their brightness

from her eyes and

sparrows use her voice

for their morning song.

Brooks take note as she flows

forward in style and grace:

Sweet serenity.

Good Morning Heaven-Sent Dream

Not to be lost in the maze of midnight pondering,

THE REST OF NIGHT CAN BRING FORTH ANYTHING

DELICATE AND PRECIOUS:

I FIND YOU AT MY THOUGHT POST,

RESTING COMFORTABLY,

"good morning, heaven, sweet dreams!"

The Blossom

The blossom is that
middle part.

It is that
center portion,
which creates the essence of a flower.

The blossom is what grows.

Thus, it can be an extension
which provides the viewer with a treat.

The blossom is the truth.

It is that real thought about what life
is all about,
showing the world how to live.

She is the blossom
of our soul and spirit,
and we need her dearly.

Warmth Remembered

Warmth carries with it a certain vitality.

A smile blankets that glimpse at hope can change life itself…

Warmth brings these things into focus.

A smile can warm the soul,

A glimmer can warm a pathway,

A hope can warm a dream,

And change can warm a heart.

Warmth remembered

can smile at those whose path has been the unlit,

and whose dreams have been interrupted.

With piercing consciousness, it can heal a soul

which has been harmed.

Wake

Wake me from my daydream

and give me a night of images,

whose emptiness will soon vanish.

Wake me from a dream into your world

that I may know

what happiness is.

We Knew Each Other

We knew each other a billion years before the oceans roared.

As a butterfly landing on my windowsill

and entering my home

as an angel, she arrived.

With the warmth, humility, charm paralleled only by the sun,

she came.

We knew each other a billion years before the oceans roared,

before cool summer breezes carried honeysuckle on their

wings, and before moonlit midnights embraced the skies.

Sweet Essence

I smell your essence on my breath.

Your fragrance rests gently
on my mind
and strokes my feelings.

The taste and smell
of you
reminds me of the beginning of time.

As I sleep
and am carried into the slumber
of this evening,
I carry you with me.

Magic Touch

I felt like waves crashing against hard
and impersonal rocks,
crashing and retreating with each effort,
feeling no release from the grips of harshness.

I had known of this ending, I had heard them say,
"do not travel there, there is no hope in that
Distant shore,"
Yet my sense casted be onward, on the path to your realm,
To your space.

The only thing that they did not tell me is how
Wonderful it would be.

Having Met You is Sufficient

Having met you

is quite sufficient

to satisfy my hunger

and thirst for loveliness.

A thought,

a smell,

a moment in your presence;

A step in your path,

next to you were fine.

I am fulfilled with your grace and charm.

You are a blessing

and good wishes are sufficient.

Prose

This prose is as perfect as I get.

I feel this lineage begins here.

These are not my thoughts:

These are not my marks:

These are not my possessions:

They are merely a representation

of what I have been allowed to do.

This prose is yours and for you.

The reader makes it and thus it is.

Only you define these words.

This prose is as perfect as I get.

Pasta Gravy

With my head held on a tilt
in cupped hands,
I stare into the red gravy,
the ceiling fan above strobes the light above it and I see my
past reflected
in the sauce
with each flicker.

The light seems to remind me of the good fortune
and the shadows of the misfortune.

I have failed as a lover,
and now as I attempt this prose,
I feebly try to express myself
and feebly my thoughts turn to carrying you
on the path to the end of time.

Wendell Pierce Breathes New Life Into Death of a Salesman

By Ken Mask

In the beginning was the word—and it was good.

Then came Arthur Miller's *Death of a Salesman*—and the word was better.

Death of a Salesman is widely considered among the greatest plays ever by an American playwright.

The story of Willy Loman, his put-upon, loving wife and his two ne'er-do-well sons has resonated with theatergoers since its debut in 1949. After opening night, *New York Daily News* theater critic John Chapman called it "Unforgettable... All is right and nothing is wrong."

And he wrote that without having seen Wendell Pierce as the lead actor.

It's hard to imagine a more powerful, controlled, nuanced performance of the overwhelmed paterfamilias than Pierce's.

Heavyweights from Lee J. Cobb, who was the original Willy, through Dustin Hoffman, Brian Dennehy and George C. Scott have all put their interpretation into poor Willy and all have been justifiably acclaimed. I've seen some of those performances from my couch via the magic of the internet and they were incredible, but it's hard to imagine anyone bringing more to the role than Pierce.

So you've seen it before, know the story backward and forward, can't imagine anyone excelling what has come before?

Well, step right this way.

My son and I made our way to Broadway, navigated the concrete jungle where the neon lights are bright even in the middle of the day—and arrived at the Hudson Theater.

In the interest of full disclosure, I admit that Pierce is a dear friend of mine. Even if I didn't know him, though, I'd say that he captains the current Broadway presentation of *Death of a Salesman* with startling vibrancy.

That is a conclusion seconded by most critics who've seen his performance.

His "Willy" has been aptly described as strong, weak and vulnerable. His baritone rises to magnificent heights and plunges to despairing lows. After one performance, I asked him how it felt portraying one of the most coveted male roles in Broadway history.

"This is not only the highlight of my career," he told me, "but the highlight of my life – the distillation of my life's work coming together in a cathartic moment of epiphany."

His performance is ably supported by Sharon D. Clarke, who plays wife Linda, and sons Khris Davis as Biff and McKinley Belcher III as Happy. They make up the central family and take the audience on a rollercoaster odyssey of post-depression 1940s economic uncertainty.

The subtle opening with Linda waiting for her husband to come home sets the stage. She is hopeful and patient, awaiting the impending, invariable angst. Willy arrives, two suitcases in tow, metaphorically representing before and after, life and impending death.

"It's all right. I came back."

Those are the first words he—with world-weary resignation—speaks.

However, nothing prepares you for the wonderfully pulsed, heart-wrenching, tear-jerking performance Pierce delivers. Along the way, you pull for Loman to break free of his psychoses. You pull for him to regain professional competence and to make it in the face of ageism and paternal disappointment.

Here is a father who wants only the best for everyone around him. He is a horticulturist. He wants to be responsible for the growth and development of those around him; to prune and to water and to fertilize, even as his own dreams wither on the vine.

Director Miranda Crowell expertly uses space and taps into the strengths of each actor. Her efforts demonstrate no anxiety to impress; the play is wonderfully paced with dangling drop down set designs for various scenes, and her strobe pictorials add flavor to Willy's dream states. Andre De Shield's "Ben" – bejeweled and immaculate in his white-on-white, international man of mystery suits—is poetic and strong as he tauntingly beckons Willy to join him in his pursuit of riches in the jungle.

The highs of Pierce's hopes and the lows of his dashed dreams are excellent, terrific reminders of our own. This is what art does, it portrays our world with intensely precise mirrors.

In the beginning was the word—and it was good.

In the hands of Miller and Pierce, it is better.

The play ends its run January 15, but it's a certainty that it will be back.

Like Willy.

Previously published in: https://www.thesaundersreport.com/post/wendell-pierce-breathes-new-life-into-death-of-a-salesman, January 13, 2023.

Pure Life Theater's Production Of August Wilson's Fences *Is Gone, But Stay Tuned For Its Return*

By Ken Mask

There's something about the combination of great writing and great acting that makes a night out at the theater refreshing.

Thomasi McDonald as Troy in August Wilson's Pulitzer and Tony winning play *Fences* provided such an occasion. With a comfortable posture he's able to bring the essence of family and human dynamics to your attention.

The literal fence and metaphoric adjustments become a superbly woven life fabric as Troy navigates his past, present and future. The uncertainty that typically comes from a poor education and the pain of a past life in prison does not sway him from his mission to take care of those around him. In the role of a garbage collector, buddy, family man and wayward husband in 1950s Pittsburgh, McDonald flows across the stage delivering Wilson's lines with splendid vitality to an everyman set of situations.

Connie Lea, as his wife Rose, delivers good humor and humility. As the loving homemaker, you could just smell the love-infused fried chicken, biscuits and collards. Later, when she got fed up, you could feel her pain as she delivered her spit-in-your-face-18-year-marriage soliloquy—the one Viols Davis made famous in the movie. Lea went toe-to-toe in matching her intensity and anguish.

Jay Randall as Cory plays the teenage angst in solid fashion, while Benaiah Barnes was solid as Troy's grown first son.

Mia Burton is a rising star; her stage presence was animated and her memorization of the father's songs and phrases was delightful.

Gabriel, Vincent Drayton, reminds us that war often goes on well beyond the battlefield. The brain-injured brother with trumpet in hand shows August Wilson's chops for contemporary commentary. Drayton's Gabe is well played with uncomfortably appropriate positioning. Ajani Kambon's Bono as Troy's best friend and coworker is on point with comedic relief and as an intermittent moral compass.

One could tell that director Jamal Farrar took full advantage of the excellent talent pool. I'm hopeful this 'takes to the road' and please bring Deb Royals's well-appointed set along. I'll drive the U-Haul just to hang with the troupe.

Thomasi McDonald is a major thespian force. Like a band leader he conducts his fellow cast members with metronome-like precision. Their timing is perfect, their pace is like a well-oiled grandfather clock up to and through the death challenge moments…all draw you in before you realize it.

[Ed. Note: The night I attended the play, the purest evidence of McDonald's mastery of the role was provided by the soto voce comments of women in the audience. Angered by the character's philandering, some women called him out of his name. The hatred toward him was palpable, when one audience member called him the 12-letter big kahuna of cusswords, I was lmost tempted to turn and tell her "You know he's just acting, right?" But I was scared.]

Wilson, the bard of our past century, was surely pleased last night from his front row seat in Heaven. The next time Pure Life puts on this production—as it invariably must—make sure you're on the front row of your local theater.

Previously published in https://www.thesaundersreport.com/post/pure-life-theater-s-production-of-august-wilson-s-fences-is-gone-but-stay-tuned-for-its-return, August 30, 2022.

The Grandma
A Three Act Play
Written by Ken Mask

The Cast

MELVIN LOUIS JENKINS
GRANDMA JENKINS

FELICIA JENKINS
BRICELYN JENKINS
TIM JOHNSON
REVEREND JONES

REVEREND'S WIFE
STEPHANIE
THE PAINTING
GOSPEL SINGING (PUBLIC DOMAIN SELECTIONS)

Setting

The setting is the living room, side porch, and small yard of the JENKINS home on a busy street. It is a two-story, wood-frame house in Durham, North Carolina—an older, well-appointed place with a simple, middle-income style. A doorway, upstage right, leads onto a porch that hosts potted plants, a few chairs, and an outdoor writer's workstation. To the left is the partially opened door to the master bedroom. In the upstage left corner is a small hallway leading to the kitchen. In the right foreground sits a sofa, coffee table, and a couple of dining tray tables. Situated on the left is a TV stand with an old, non-smart television. Books line the lower shelf of the TV stand and the adjacent bookshelves. Windows line the right wall; paintings rest on the floor on either side of the windows.

People are still reeling from the post-COVID climate, facing uncertainty on many levels. Jobs are plentiful, but there is a restless energy in the air. As always—but now seemingly more than ever—networking and personal connections are the most reliable pathways to success.

Children, particularly teenagers, are more comfortable expressing themselves to both peers and adults, bolstered by the clarity and assertiveness shaped by modern technology. They are aware and self-assured. However, social media has complicated the art of real-world interaction, often making it feel awkward or forced.

The challenges of an aging population affect everyone. Most Black families typically don't place grandparents in nursing homes. Instead, if they are able, they take turns caring for their elders at home.

Act 1

Act 1, Scene 1

It is summer 2024. A family consisting of father, mother and daughter begin an evening meal.

{Music-public domain spirituals}

As the curtain rises, MELVIN, 60 years old, FELICIA, 50 and their daughter BRICE, 17 get ready for a meal. Melvin, a solidly built African American, careful and deliberate in motion but not stoic is an assistant editor of City Gazette which is on its way out. They recently announced that it is going solely online.

He has a bit of anxiety about potentially not being employed in a few months and may have to fall back on carpentry from an earlier career. Felicia feisty and full bodied dark mocha chocolate with a self assured poster, pretty with bright doe eyes is a substitute high school teacher. Her passion work is interior decorating; the largest clients are developers who stage homes for phase community sells. Brice is slightly chubby with no anxiety to impress, a high school student with a fierce attitude in general and good spirits but holds a secret.

The three sit next to each other on a sofa and watch a sporting event on TV. It plays quietly in the background. They eat on three separate small dinner tray tables. Game food, chips, sodas, candy items are scattered on the coffee table. A conversation continues.

MELVIN: Between here, JoJo and Mae. Not long.....You've done a great job here Felicia; making it home for moms

FELICIA: Anything for your mom dear. Anything.

BRICE: Why is she here so much? All she does is sit and sit and take up space. Auntie and them got that big ole house.

MELVIN: Have, Mae and they 'have' a big ole house.

FELICIA: Don't entertain her Mel. Hush. I told you about saying that Brice! Your grandmother keeps this family together.
MELVIN: Your mother's right. Didn't we tell you about this kinda comment?

BRICE: You tell me a lot, mostly nonsense. And it's 'kind of.' And she keeps this family together, just how?

FELICIA: That'll get you some belt young lady.

BRICE: Some belt? Yeah, right. I'm a big girl...just'll turn you in to protection services.

FELICIA: Told you, they can have you.

MELVIN. Yes. I'll pack your things.
(He puts the tray on the coffee take and stands)

BRICE. Not funny dad.

FELICIA: What you say about your grandmother is not funny Brice. Melvin, sit down. This joke is old.

MELVIN. Maybe Some belt then?

BRICE: Bring it on mister. (They laugh)

FELICIA: I'll fix your mother's plate and bring it to her.

MELVIN: Okay. Thank you Felicia. You know she's watchin the game. Better wait 'til the quarter's over.

BRICE: Why she watching a NBA game?

FELICIA: 'An.'

BRICE: And what?

EVELVIN: Why is she watching 'an' NBA game. Not a.

BRICE: Anyway, she like what 90?

FELCIA. Why are you so disrespectful. Your grandmother is 92. Show some decency.

MELVIN: She's been a fan since Elgin Baylor.

BRICE: Who? Y'all know I'm kidding about granny. She and I are cuts.

FELICIA: Look him up.

BRICE: I would if I had an iPhone like my friends.

MELVIN: So you do know correct diction when you need to...

Felicia motions to the kitchen. She grabs Melvin's empty plate and tray. The is a LOUD THUMB coming from the bedroom.
MELVIN: Mommma (He knocks over Brice's dinner tray upon standing and arrives into the bedroom in urgent fashion.)

GRANDMOTHER: The strong, bright eyed, solidly alert 92 year old is on the floor, next to the double bed. She lays prone, legs folded up into a fetal position.

(Beat)

BRICE: Granny!
She has entered the bedroom and is near her dad.

FELICIA:(In the door frame with a towel and ice) Are you Okay?

GRANDMOTHER: I'm okay. Just putting my things up. Did Y'all pray before you ate?

MELVIN: We've told you to call us mamma. Whenever you need anything...............And, no we didn't.

BRICE: Nope!

FELICIA: Are you Sure she's ok darling?

MELVIN: I Think so.

GRANDMOTHER: Clucks her teeth. I change your diapers boy.

They laugh.

MELVIN: Oh I know. You've told me a million times. And, its you 'changed' my diapers.

FELICIA: Ya, she's good!

GRANDMOTHER: Still do. And Shirley Mae's and Jojo's .(they laugh) And all them white folk's kids. Before I saved up enough money to put myself through college. Them gals never wanted to take care of the babies. Too busy with their new appliances and all. Ice boxes, cars, fancy clothes.

MELVIN: They know it too; and them mommas; at least I hope they do remember- a college girl helping them! But certain folk have short memories of kindness.

GRANDMOTHER: You got that right babbbby. But the Lord forgives.

MELVIN: Yes yes...But that's got nothing to do with you trying to be Hercules now. The 1950s were the 1950s and now we in a new time. Ice boxes?

GRANDMOTHER: How you know?

MELVIN: I've heard your stories from Pops. - It's the second quarter and the Lakers are up by 20.

They laugh. Brice stands in the doorway, arms crossed.

GRANDMOTHER: That LeBron! Test-tube-baby!

MELVIN: How do you know that? And just what do you know about a test tube baby?

GRANDMOTHER. I'm old, not dead! (giggles)Your daddy and I loved us some Robin Harris.

MELVIN: Get some sleep momma. I'm going out to the porch to finish this working on this article

GRANDMOTHER: When's your deadline?

MELVIN: Tomorrow, early AM.

GRANDMA: Okay darling. Please turn off that box and turn that little light on. I'm gonna read a bit from the GOOD BOOK.

BRICE:(Who has entered the room.) The box? And. ....
What about Islam
or Buddha?

MELVIN: That's enough Brice.

GRANDMOTHER: Same SUPREME BEING, Lyn.
(rolls eyes)

Melvin kisses his mother on the forehead; he and Brice return back into the living room.

MELVIN: Why you want to rib your grandmother?

BRICE: She likes it. It's our little thing.

MELVIN: Sometimes your mother doesn't get it.

FELICIA: Get what?

MELVIN: That what Brii says about mom is just jousting.

FELICIA: I'm not stupid. Do you think she wants to eat?
(She places the plate on the table)

MELVIN: We had a fairly big and late lunch. JOJO brought over some ribs and potato salad, sweet tea, rolls.

FELICIA: Well I'm surprised she let him out. That brother of yours is straight whipped and beat down.

MELVIN: Okay, alright now. (laughs)
They sit to watch some of the game. Brice stands, grabs a knapsack, motions to exit the front door.

MELVIN: Where is she going?

FELICIA: Just across the street. Stephanie is studying and asked her...

MELVIN: Huh. To what help?
He motions toward the front door and opens.

MELVIN: School night Brii. Home by 11.

BRICE: Okay dad. (from the yard)

FELICIA: She's good in math Mel. You know that.

MELVIN: Yeah. Just want her to be all she can be. Is she good at her OWN math?

FELICIA: Plus, she doesn't have many friends and lucky that Step is right there; this neighborhood. ..... she wants to be a lawyer but know she
needs math.

MELVIN: Yeah. Mmm huh. Why does she say those things about momma?

The game has resumed and he, sits, grabs the remote; turns up the volume.

FELICIA: You know she likes to kid around...they are tight Mel. Tight and right...

TV ANNOUNCER: Lakers are ON tonight! Crowd noise.

FELICIA: I'll take her plate and put it in the frig.

She passes by the bedroom and peeks in.

MELVIN: Let me guess, fast asleep?

FELICIA: Nope, fast praying.

MELVIN: Mmm huh.

FELICIA: I'll knock out these dishes.

MELVIN: I'll do the pots.

FELICIA: You got it, babbbbbby
She is there for a while and returns, again peering into the room.

FELICIA. Whew!

MELVIN: What.
(He stands) Is She ok?

FELICIA: Still on them knees Mel.

MELVIN. Yup. But wait.
(He rises again, looking at the clock on the wall) He rushes to the bedroom door and pauses, staring.

MELVIN: Okay. I can see her prayer strut.

FELICIA: Strut?

MELVIN: Ask Mae.

It's subtle. They return to the living room sofa. (Beat)

The two hug; she rubs his belly. He rubs her hair.

FELICIA: Ice cream?

MELVIN: Why not, nobody's keeping score. I can dip some of the Snickers into the bowl.

He reaches for some of the game food, he grabs a few bars on the way out toward the kitchen and peers in again into the bedroom.

FELICIA: They're keeping score of that game. And I'm keeping score of your weight. Notorious.

MELVIN: Hehehehehehe, . You!

He peers into the bedroom.

MELVIN: Dang.

FELICIA: What? Still?...But for real..I give about a 14 second prayer, and in the bed not on my knees.

MELVIN. Reach me my phone.
(She grabs the phone from an nearby charger stand and hands it to him)

He takes a picture of his mother praying.

End of Act 1 Scene 1

Act 1 Scene 2

{Music-defer to our director}

It is the next morning. The living room coffee table has been cleared of the game party items. The tv dinner tables host breakfast items. The TV is on. GOSPEL RADIO SINGING is heard from the bedroom; it is pleasant and non-intrusive. Someone sings along, not grandma. The voice is harmonious and strong without being overbearing. Felicia arranges the food on the tables. Melvin turns on the TV.

MELVIN. This is fine for what we need. Huh, smart TVs? Smart phones? What's next, smart cars?

FELICIA: They have them now Melvin. Self driving, The cars drive themselves

MELVIN: Nope not me, I'm keeping ME in charge of my car. Good solid Betsy. I'm not ever trusting a car to drive for me!

There is a knock at the door.
FELICIA: I'll get it. (She moves toward the front door and peers out of the peep hole).

MELVIN: Let me guess, T?

FELICIA: Yes.

TIM JOHNSON enters through the door that Felicia leaves open with the posture of the frequent visitor. He is awkward

86

in motion, in his 40s, a graduate at the Greensboro College of Arts (or can wear a Sweatshirt of a college of director's choice; can't find work and hasn't sold 'real
paying' painting in years. He lives here and there most times, but recently found a border type set up that requires the tenants to work real jobs. enters from outside, behind Tim.

BRICE: The fat starving artist! Looking for breakfast with your broke- ass?

MELVIN: That's not right...Hehehehehe. But hey little girl, I'm the only one who can rib him this early!

TIM: Jokes.... Y'all treat me so bad. Especially you Lynn!

FELICIA: Knew you'd be coming. I'll get you some of these pancake and grits.

TIM: Cheesy grits?

MELVIN: Boy, you really are country!

TIM: You too, bud.

BRICE: And, Granny's the only one who can call me Lynn!

(She exits heading into the kitchen.)

Melvin reaches for a chess board beneath the table.

MELVIN: Come on and get this ass whipping.

TIM: Set emup.

MELVIN: You must Owe rent? Let's bet. You got any cash.

TIM: Way past. You got my paintings there.

He looks over to the stack near the front window; he turns to Felicia.

TIM: Are there any development projects coming? Would really love to place these in staging models.

MELVIN: You are Going to need cash and more than that for rent and things. How.....

TIM: You know the art world!
He looks again to Felicia who is preparing food.

TIM: I'm not cut out for regular work. I guess, like father like son!

MELVIN: Don't talk to me about absent fathers.

Felicia puts her hand on her hips and shakes her head. Melvin thinks the gesture is for him.

FELICIA: That's your problem.

TIM: Art world's a hard row to ho.

MELVIN: Didn't you know that? like 15 years ago when you got that degree?

TIM: Wish I had a skill like you; people always need a clown.

MELVIN: Oh I Got cha clown right here. (They laugh.)

FELICIA: Mind your manners. And your paintings... there... well, need a dust buster. They could use a good dusting.

She looks toward Brice, then the paintings on the floor near the window and tosses her head for the two men to head out to the porch. They get it and motion to leave, but added conversation...

TIM: Fel - Surely you have some upcoming staging gigs with Phillips- Jones -Humphries? Didn't they just break ground in three locations?

MELVIN: That cuts deep; a 'clown' huh? They call me the Bard. Could go back to carpentry though and plug into that development flow... mmm huh!

TIM: Yes yes

MELVIN: When I can find work. And ya know the writing gig at the Gazette is fading; online version coming and we are all on pins...rag won't last past the Fall. Yup, online content and AI...

TIM: You know the Immigrants are taking all the jobs right?

FELICIA: Don't let granny hear that kind of talk! That's some of the damnest shit you can say. Shouldn't feed your monkey-ass. You two are meant for each other. You had that kinda language back at the center...and well.

The stove alarms the food is reasy- she exits to the kitchen to get food for Tim.

TIM: You know I'm kidding. Don't tell momma. As Mark Twain said: "If I do not get out of debt....pistols or poison for me!"

Melvin sets up the chess board. Tim hustles to the TV dinner table begins to scarf down the food.

FELICIA: Slow down. Dang. Brice was right. You're not a starving artist; your ribs ain't showing.

(They laugh.)

TIM: Okay. Okay. Good. Oh, AND did you speak with that gallery cross town?

FELICIA: Will do. Okay. Got cha.

Tim: (Tim's Phone rings) Hello, yes, right now? Be right there. Sorry folks, hate to eat and run but I need to chase down this paper. Later. (rushes out the door.)

Melvin: Hey, but what about this butt whooping I was about to give on this chess board? Beat... I sure will be glad when he starts making some real money.

Felicia: Melvin, can I see that picture you took again?

Melvin: Sure (Melvin takes out phone pulls up picture and hands it to Felicia)

Felicia: (Studies the picture) beat...I have an idea, Tim is a good painter right?

Melvin: Yes he is, when he puts his mind to it.

Felicia: Then why don't you commission him to paint a portrait of this picture as
a gift for your mom. You know he needs the money and I think this is something he could "put his mind to it".

Melvin: Yeah, but I don't know about that. I really don't like doing business with friends. Especially friends like Tim.

Felicia: Just think about it. You would give him a reason to be serious about his work and make some money at the same time.

Melvin: You got a point. I'll think about it

FELICIA: Back when we were at the gallery space Tim ha some rough spots.

Melvin: Yup. Should I take it easy on him on the chess game.

(Laughs)

(Studies the board)

FELICIA: I'm serious Mel.

Melvin: Me too, (Laughs). Turns serious. You helped him out quite a bit.

FELICIA: Don't know....

End of Act 1, Scene 2

Act 1, Scene 3

It is next week, Wednesday evening. A buzzing collection of Bible toting REVEREND JONES, HIS WIFE, arrive on the porch of the Jenkins home. Grandma meets them on the front door, opens it.

GRANDMA: Bible study! Yes yes ! Hallelujah! Welcome.

{Music}

(A song breaks out among the deaconesses. "We are climbing Jacobs Ladder" is started by one lady. Others chime in.)

WIFE1: We are climbing Jacobs' ladder, We are climbing Jacobs' ladder...We are climbing Jacob' ladder...

REVEREND: : Soldiers of the cross...

Every round goes higher, higher Every round goes higher, higher Every rung goes higher, higher, Soldiers of the cross...

GRANDMA: (solo) Sinner, do you, love my Jesus? Sinner, do you, love my Jesus? Sinner, do you, love my Jesus? Soldiers of the cross.

They enter the home and take seats in the living room. Bryce Felicia and Melvin grab chairs from the other rooms to accommodate the group.

REVEREND JONES: You know with all this pandemic, covid stuff going around, We haven't had Bible study in a while. Sister Jenkins it was nice of you to invite us to your home...And IT IS refreshing to. We are here today after a long time. The time has been long but the strength of the Lord is longer .COVID came and COVID went, or so we hope so. We lost some folk and some folk still are with us.

PREACHER'S WIFE: Amen

REVEREND JONES: But the goodness is strong and strong is the goodness of the Lord. His SON shines on us like the sun in the almighty sky shining through trees and landing on the good green soil. And we, my friends are the soil.

PREACHER'S WIFE: Amen Rev, amen.

REV. JONES: I'd like to invite Ms Jenkins, the matriarch of the Jenkins family to lead tonight's study.

(Grandma slowly comes up to the center of the room.)

GRANDMA: (She slowly opens her Bible)Well Thank you reverend Today's STUDY comes from the Gospel Luke. The good doctor. The one who has the job of healing the sick and curing the illnesses of the day. The sick look to the doctor and the doctor looks to the Lord.
WIFE: Well.

GRANDMA: Taste and See that the Lord is good, Oh the joys of those who take refuse in HIM, Psalm 34:8

BRICE: Or HER.

DEACON 3: Okay now.

REVEREND JONES: Amen young sister Jenkins. Amen. Your grandma I see is in the house. Great to see you Sister Jenkins.

REVEREND JONES: And the good Lord, like mother earth takes care of her children

GRANDMA: What Luke is telling us is that the Lord, as a HE or SHE in '23. Like Michael Jordan, is the truth! On this court of life and like Jordan, in the last shot you can count on GOOOOOOOOODDDDDDD to have your points. You can count on that being a good shot. And that shot wins games and the games of life are full and righteous for those to turn their heart and the thoughts to the Lord in sincere and just trust. (Beat) Let "the church" (PHRASE) say AMEN.

WIFE: Or Lebron!
They laugh.

GRANDMA: And the way that we listen to the Lord is to pray and to seek. We turn to this goodness with open hearts and open minds with prayer and we talk to the Lord.

WIFE: Yes yes. And that's right.

GRANDMA: We have the direct line. And the direct line allows us to speak with our most sincere thoughts.
Just as the Lord entrusted Joseph with the care of his child, he entrusts this world to each of us.

WIFE: Amen.

GRANDMA: And when Joseph was entrusted with the care of Jesus, he was chosen for this assignment. And you must ask yourself, like I asked myself this morning. Would I have picked Joseph. And I must say no.
Joseph was not a Rabbi. Joseph did not live in the best neighborhood. Joseph was not the educated man of the times with a large amount of money. How would he provide for this new SON? But GOD knew!
He knew Joseph was meek and kind. He knew that Joseph was decent and accepted the assignment to protect the honor of his new wife.

REV: Well. Well. Amen.

GRANDMA: And GOD KNEW Joseph was masterful. Masterful enough to instruct his son, Jesus on the ways of the world. To work hard and to be kind. AND GOD KNEW that Joseph was humble. Humble enough to know and to trust in the new situation. Humble to take this unbelievable denouncement from his dream to BELIEVE. Sometimes we need to put down our EGO AND TO ACCEPT THE things that come our way. To be ready for the unknown and to TRUST in the Lord. HE or SHE, Ms young Jenkins, DARLING.

BRYCE: Amen, Amen. (sarcastic)

OTHERS laugh.

GRANDMA: What we have at the end of the day is
HUMILITY, MERCIFUL WAYS AND MASTERY. Joseph
was humble and kind. Joseph as indicated in LUKE turned
to the LORD. And he was merciful. He took care of his
new wife to protect her dignity. He took time to listen and
most of all he was masterful; he knew that the saviour
of the world needed instruction. The instruction was what
we need; to pass on the knowledge that we have and to
share.

(Grandma stands to return to another chair and becomes

FAINT. Melvin and Bryce, others rush to help.)

Curtain falls End of Act 1

Act 2

Act 2, Scene 1

Afternoon, the next day. The Jenkins living room. The four, Melvin, Felicia, Brice and Grandma take seats on the sofa and adjacent chairs. A conversation continues:

FELICIA: A fainting spell; blood rushes from your head.

BRICE: Ah, okay. Seems fine?

MELVIN: More like the Holy Ghost.

BRICE: Ah, what?

MELVIN: You know the feeling of goose bumps; when something special happens; say for instance a good scene in a movie touches you or a cool moment with friends makes you warm and tingling? The greatness of the Lord can do that; when you realize that things are ok and the chord strikes you in a most joyous instance; you get goosebumps on your arms and the currents of pleasure give you assurance that everything is in place: THAT CAN BE the HOLY GHOST- a sense of pleasure in the presence of truth, gratitude.

GRANDMA: That is your wonderful writing style ML! Brilliantly put.

BRICE: Okay.

GRANDMA: I was moved. I asked: did you all pay attention to the Rev or were you daydreaming?

BRICE: Daydreaming.

GRANDMA: A dream is just a dream without a plan.

BRICE: Hehehehehehhe . You got that right granny. Be sure to tell Tim when he comes.

FELICIA: Tim?

BRICE: You know he's coming for something to eat.

MELVIN: Now-now Brii . Don't you have homework to do?

There is a knock at the door.

FELICIA: Psychic.

GRANDMA: Psychotic. They laugh. Felicia goes to the door.

TIM: Hey now.
She leaves the door ajar and he enters. There is paint on his hand and clothes.

FELICIA: Go wash up Tim.

MELVIN: I'll get some towels. You don't wash up at your place.

TIM: Not there. Out.

FELICIA: Again?

GRANDMA: There's some rubbing alcohol in the kitchen. Get that Tim.

She get up to motion to the kitchen. The others remain in the living room.

TIM: Yes ma.

MELVIN: Yes.

FELICIA: Speaking of paint...Mel did you show Tim that picture of your mom praying?

BRICE: Praying?

FELICIA: Oh. It's a secret.

MELVIN: Yes. I will explain.

There is another knock at the door.

FELICIA: Any idea who this is Brii?

BRICE: Haha. It's Step mom, we're going to study!

MELVIN: Study or do makeup?

BRICE: Everybody's a comedian. Am I missing something?

BRICE: You always miss something.

TIM: Haha.

FELICIA: She guessed it was you at the door before you knocked.

TIM: And, said something bad?

MELVIN: Not anything out of the ordinary.

TIM: Loves her jousting matches.

Brice has opened the door. STEPHANIE, 20s-30s year old (director's casting choice) strides with confidence of a close friend, enters; bookstack on back.

STEPHANIE: Hi all. Even you Tim.

TIM: It's Mr. Johnson young lady. .

STEPHANIE: Right. (laughs)

FELICIA: What's that suppose to mean?

STEPHANIE: I used to work down at the Arts Center, before COVID and nametags were mandatory; yada yada yada . Now back in school. Community College...lucky to have Brii-Brri across the street,

TIM: Hierarchy. Rank. Rank is important.

FELCIA: I like that. Society has gotten away from respect.

GRANDMA: Society has gotten away from the LORD!

TIM: Amen.

MELVIN: Amen.

Melvin and Tim follow Felicia to the kitchen. Stephanie, Brice and Grandma remain.

GRANDMA: What are you two studying.

STEPHANIE: Math.

BRICE: Calc.

GRANDMA: 1 or 2?

STEPHANIE: That's funny. What do you know about calculus?

GRANDMA: Took it with Einstein. They laugh.

BRICE: Hear from dad you were good in math?

GRANDMA: Good enough to help him, your aunt Shirley Mae and Joseph with anything they were doing. Plus had quite a bit at BENNETT in the 50's.

STEPHANIE: Thought you studied music?

GRANDMA: Yes, piano.

STEPHANIE: Do you still play?

GRANDMA: (reminiscing) Haven't played in a long time.

BRICE: Athur's rittus
.

They laugh; including Grandma. Brice and Stephanie turn to leave the room.

GRANDMA: Study long but don't study wrong.

BRICE: Good one granny. You still got it.

GRANDMA: Think I'll take a nappypoo
.

She motions to the bedroom.
TIM: So tell me about this picture.

MELVIN: So, here is the deal. I took this picture of mom praying and Felicia thought it might be a good idea if I paid you to do a portrait of it. What do you think>

MELVIN: Here.

He takes out his cell phone and shows the picture.

TIM: Wow, that's Deep. He continues to study the picture.

FELICIA: And this can be a magnificent gift...

MELVIN: Ah great; yes yes. (.They all peer at the picture.) Of course it would a commissioned piece, I think I want to name it ahhhhhh ahhh Let me see, THE PRAYING GRANDMA.

FELICIA: Get Tim to do a painting1 Text it to him; that is if his phone is working.

MELVIN: Ahh, Yes, Great idea. After all, all of our successes and accomplishments are usually not our doing. These items come from the deep hard work of folk who pray for us.

TIM: Preach! And, you better get a print out of this at FEDEX.

MELVIN: You know she had us in church three times a week for 17 years.

TIM: Or at least on Sundays!

FELICIA: She'd love this.

MELVIN: And we could have an unveiling at Bennett.

TIM: And, around town, or at least at the church.

FELICIA: The church you don't attend?

MELVIN: Now now, don't go there,

.TIM: I need this.

MELVIN: Ah...You do?

TIM: Rents due, past due. And....

MELVIN: Hold up, I said I'll commission you not retire you!

They laugh. We'll have to alter the background and add some things to the room to make it really click.

TIM: Okay. Like?

MELVIN: Like add her Bible, the big one in the closet on the table. Here. And the background. I'll have to think about...
He points to the picture.

TIM: Okay.

MELVIN: And perhaps add a picture of the church down home way on the wall, here.

FELICIA: Like, like. This is wonderful. I'm so excited!!

TIM: Immah need some supplies.

MELVIN: Man, You always broke! Lets talk money, I will pay you in advance. (they exit, blackout)

Act 2, Scene 2

The Jenkins home, living room. It is midday. Melvin and Felicia sit on the sofa. Grandma is in the bedroom.

There is a knock at the door. Grandma asks from the bedroom.

GRANDMA: Who's there?

MELVIN: We're right here mom. No worries.

He motions toward the door. Tim pauses on the porch.

TIM: Whispers through the cracked door. I've got some work done cuz.

MELVIN: On what? Oh. Stay there. I'll come out.

FELICIA: (Yells) Tell him there's no food.
They laugh.

MELVIN: (Whispers to Felicia) Tim Says he has some work done on the painting.

PAINTING WHICH IS COVERED WITH A CANVAS

Tim and Melvin move onto the porch. Tim shows the large canvas to Melvin. The audience cannot see.

MELVIN: Woooohwweeeee

TIM: Mmmm; I thought you'd like it.

(Beat)

MELVIN: Huh?

TIM: Huh what?

MELVIN: Looks great. But I've got a couple of suggestions..

TIM: Suggestions? Okay. But I thought I was the artist. What are your suggestions.

MELVIN: Let me see. Let's change the background, it don't pop. I don't like the wall and the table.

TIM: Okay, I can do that.

MELVIN: Cool.

Felicia has come out to the porch. Tim and Melvin grab the painting and turn it.

MELVIN: Hold up not yet. Only the artists can see the work.

FELICIA: I can respect that....

Tim motions to remove the painting from the area and places a canopy over it. Stephanie has arrived.

STEPHANIE: Okay. What's up y'all?

MELVIN: Special project for my mom.

STEPHANIE: Ah. Okay. I got cha. Cool. Cool. (Beat) how sweet. Brii home?

FELICIA: She's not back yet?

STEPHANIE: (upset) Back from where?

MELVIN: Practice. Kicking that ball around like a true champ.

STEPHANIE: I know...mmmm huh... I'll stop back by later.

Tim motions to leave. Stephanie follows, in a noisy posture; trying to get a lookay. She gently eases up to Tim as they exit the porch. Melvin goes back in. The two, Tim and Stephanie sit.

TIM: Hey, lookay. Immah tell you but it's a secret.

STEPHANIE: A painting is a secret? I've been a fan of yours since the center days.

TIM: Yes, you see Melvin snapped a picture of his mother praying.

STEPHANIE: Cool. And?

TIM: He commissioned me to do a painting of his picture.

STEPHANIE: Ahhhh . And... ahhh Mmmmm

TIM: What?

STEPHANIE: Well how you gonna make money? It's yours right.

TIM: Well no, not actually, it's a commissioned piece. He's paying me to paint it. Already given me some of the money.

He shows her the WHITE ENVELOPE of money Melvin gave him.

STEPHANIE: So. You can take this on tour. This is one of your best items Tim. Since the early days!

TIM: Yeah, I know. Let me go. I've gotta get this back to the studio and work on some things.
He leaves and she returns to the front porch. Knocks.

(beat)

Felicia comes onto the front porch.

FELICIA: I know he showed you.

STEPHANIE: Ahhh yup. Yes. Yes...it's great. But ahhhh

FELICIA: What? Let's not get to that mess you used to stir back in the day~

STEPHANIE: Well isn't the photograph the real art. I mean why not just blow it up and present it?

FELICIA: Well. Ahhh . (mockingly) Now you know what I mean...ain't the time.

STEPHANIE: Let me see it. The real art?

.

FELICIA: You mean the picture Melvin took?

STEPHANIE: Yeah the picture. But....

MELVIN COMES OUT....

They arrest their encounter.

FELICIA: Show Step the picture of ma.

He shows her the picture on his phone. They sit and study the screen.

FELICIA: Yes. Yes.

MELVIN: I just think that the art as artist is best interaction with their skill to render a work. It has more texture as an interpretation, not a snap.

STEPHANIE: Well the energy of the art is the ability to capture a moment, with the picture framed and with an eye for the moment's intensity.
He shows her the picture again on his phone. They sit and study the screen.

FELICIA EXITS.

Beat

MELVIN: Yes. Huh.

STEPHANIE: I just think that if there is some money to be made...

MELVIN: Money to be made? What are you talking about. This is a surprise gift for my mother.

STEPHANIE: Okay, I just thought.....

MELVIN: Well stop thinking!!!

End of Act 2, Scene 2

Act 2, Scene 3

Jenkins home; is later in the day. Melvin and Felicia sit at TV dinner tray tables. Bryce sits studying on the floor using the coffee table; books all over. Grandma is reading in the corner.

MELVIN: Super BLTs. I Love your afternoon snacks.

FELICIA: Thanks dear, makes for an easy cleanup.

MELVIN: I got the paper plates; cups, cans.
They laugh.

BRICE: What are you reading granny?

GRANDMA: Physics.

BRICE: Right?

MELVIN: It was her minor.

FELICIA: Yes indeed. You should've known...where you been?

BRICE: In college? Deep. You'd said Einstein.

GRANDMA: I was being funny. Ain't that old Lyn!

BRICE: But dang; physics Granny?

GRANDMA: Ahhhh yes. And music.

MELVIN: That's straight out racist Brii

FELICIA: And ageist!

BRICE: Ageist?

MELVIN: Elderly people racism.

FELICIA: Your grandmother taught high school Physics in the 70s, 80s.

MELVIN: And music.

They approach her to see the texts.

GRANDMA: American Journal of Physics. Leibniz's integral rule to calculate the variables of the Kepler problem.

BRICE: ANNNNNNNNNNNNNAAAAAAAAMMMMM.

The curtain falls. End of Act 2.

Act 3 Scene 1

Midday. The Jenkin's home. Tim arrives on the front porch. He sits and waits; hands on his forehead in thought. Stephanie arrives. It is a continuation of a conversation:

STEPHANIE: Did you give any thoughts to my suggestion.

TIM: What suggestion.

STEPHANIE: The money you can make off of this painting!!

TIM: Yeah, that. Well, I'm not sure about doing that. I told you, it's A commissioned piece. I'm not sure how I can justify keeping it.

STEPHANIE: Well. This is what you do. Explain to him that as the painter it is yours until the transfer. The transfer as assets is the only means of ownership.

TIM: But we have an agreement. I mean he gave me some bread; suppliers and a canvas.

STEPHANIE: Hell, that's a loan. Supplies are just that. Do you two have something in writing? Your studio space is cramped and you're a major artist bru with this....

TIM: Well, I just don't know.

STEPHANIE: Like second or third. Whatever. Have you ever heard of the Banjo Player by Tanner.

TIM: That's insulting Step. Of course.

STEPHANIE: Well this is like that son. The money that you can generate is huge!

TIM: Huh.

STEPHANIE: Huh my butt.
Someone approaches. There are foot steps. Stephanie motions to leave. Tim stands. They were uncomfortable is posturing.
BRYCE: What are the two of you up to? Y'all look guilty!

She laughs, breaking the tension.

STEPHANIE: Yeah now. Let's get to this work. Test in two days.

BRYCE: A snack and roll.

STEPHANIE: Bet.

She turns to Tim behind Brice with a thumbs up. Tim turns to leave.

BRYCE: Dad'll be home around soon. I Think he had a job interview.

TIM: Okay, Cool.

As he turns to leave. (Beat) Melvin arrives.

MELVIN: Hey now. What's up?

TIM: Been thinking.

MELVIN: That's always good.

They laugh. Tim leaves. Melvin enters the living room. Grandma is sitting on the sofa reading the Bible.

GRANDMA: That you Mel? Hey babbbbby

MELVIN: Hi there mama.

GRANDMA: Your girl read the Bible much?

MELVIN: None of us do; sorry.

GRANDMA: There's always prayer.

MELVIN: What do you mean?

Felicia enter the living room. Melvin pulls her to the side, stage left, near the door.

MELVIN: Whispers. Did you tell mammma about me taking a picture of her praying?

FELICIA: No. Why.

MELVIN: Nothing. She just mentioned prayer to me.

FELICIA: What else is new? She always talks about prayer.

GRANDMA: What's for dinner Fel?

FELICIA: Your greens recipe. Just like you make em

GRANDMA: Ahhh . Okay. Remember, we gonna pray before meals and for that matter before all things.

MELVIN: Yes yes
.
Grandma motions to her bedroom.

FELICIA: How's the job search.

MELVIN: Not good. But I have something coming.

FELICIA: Serious Something coming? Listen, I have to share something with you.
She takes out a notebookay.

MELVIN: What's wrong.

FELICIA: I was cleaning Brrii's room and well...

MELVIN: We said no snooping.

FELICIA: Forget that....

Bryce comes in from the front door. Felicia hides the notebook in the sofa.

BRICE: Hi....ahhhh. What's going on....?

MELVIN: Good day darling.

BRICE: What's really going on? You rarely call me daring.

FELICIA: Listen....I found this... She reaches for the notebookay.

BRICE: Are you kidding me? You've been in my ROOM!

She attempts to retrieve the item from her mom.

MELVIN: Whoa! Young lady!

Brice storms out of the front door.

End of Act 3, Scene 1

Act 3 Scene 2

Jenkins' living room. Later that evening. Melvin and Felicia sit.

MELVIN: Spells? Potions? What....

FELICIA: As long as I've known our daughter, I have never thought of this...

MELVIN: As long as you have known her?

FELICIA: I mean as a thinking person; growing up from the age of 4...she's been normal.

MELVIN: Normal?

FELICIA: Well just, ah....

MELVIN: I know. I know. But when do you think this kicked in? Let's not tell mom about this...it would kill her.

FELICIA: I agree. It wouldn't be wise. With her recent condition; of course.

MELVIN: How can WE handle this? Do you think that Stephanie has anything to do with this? What exactly are the notes?

They peer over and study the contents of the notebookay.

FELICIA: Alter of the life beneath and in the sky?

MELVIN: These diagrams are, whew!

FELICIA: What in the world? And, these drawings...here?
Reverend Jones could help!

They peruse the notebook further.

MELVIN: I don't know. We don't need this getting out!
Maybe a doctor?

There is a knock at the door. It startles them. Melvin goes
toward the front door.

TIM: Mel.................... it's me.

MELVIN: Ah. Coming. Put that in our room.

Felicia goes to the back. Tim comes in with the standard
posture but with hesitation.

MELVIN: What's wrong?

TIM: Ha. You know me.

MELVIN: You know I do, ever since we were kids! So
what's up?.

TIM: And that's why this is so hard...

MELVIN: What are you talking about T?

Tim hands him a WHITE envelope.

MELVIN: What's this?

TIM: The money you gave me for the painting.

MELVIN: Huh?

TIM: I have decided to keep ownership of the painting. As the artist, I'll keep the ownership.

MELVIN: Wait, WHAT? You're kidding me right? I don't understand? We had an agreement, an arrangement?

TIM: But nothing in writing. I spoke with an attorney, he advised me that there is no legal transfer unless we have a contract.

MELVIN: An attorney? Dude, are you freaking kidding me? What the Hell are you talking about? Where is all of this coming from.

TIM: Man look, you know I've been struggling as an artist. This some of my best work. I think I can make a lot of money off of this one painting.

MELVIN: Oh, I see. So its all about the money?

TIM: The picture you took was only a portion of the work, The artistry is from my creation. My reactions to the picture is what makes this mine and the interwoven intervals are from my creative engagement. People pray all the time.

MELVIN: Interwoven intervals, creative engagement? Yeah, you right, people do pray, and you start praying that I don't kick your ass right now?

TIM: Look, there no reason to bring violence into this. Don't you see?   I believe I can take the painting on a tour and make a lot of money.

MELVIN: We'll see about that............................ I can just take the picture, a blown up version on the tour; to sell prints and move on....

TIM: turns to leave. My mind is made up!! I'm gonna get this money

Melvin grabs him by the arm.

MELVIN: (threatening) Think the folk at First Union down home may want to talk about "money."

(beat)

TIM: Whoooooa. Damn! So you want to go there? You wouldn't? That was 20 years ago.

MELVIN: Ain't no statute of limitations on a federal crime, your son of a ….

TIM: Oh, so now you gonna do battle with me?

MELVIN: If that's what it takes.'

TIM: Never took you for a rat and a poisonous snake?

MELVIN: Wait, you calling ME a snake? I don't believe this shit? Dude, you're trying to steal my portrait!!

TIM: It's my portrait!! You just took a damn picture. This is ridiculous. You wouldn't really....

MELVIN: You wanna play this game? I can show you better than I can tell you. Watch me.

Felicia has returned. Melvin is unsure of what she overheard; he motions to bend with his hands on his knees; exhausting like resting.

Tim abruptly leaves the front door.

FELICIA: What's going on with the two of you? Old wounds?

MELVIN: You have no idea.

FELICIA: Talk to me.

MELVIN: Can you believe that son of a bitch is trying to claim my portrait? Thinks it is his best work and that he can make a lot of money putting it on tour. I told you it wasn't a good idea.

FELICIA: Yeah, but he's your friend, I can't believe he would do that.

MELVIN: Yeah, but it was your idea to pay him to paint it.

FELICIA: Don't go trying to put the blame on me!!

MELVIN: Don't worry, I got something for his ass. I gotta talk to mama.

Melvin exits to his mother's bedroom.

FELICIA: (tries to stop him) But we have to figure out what we are going to do with about Brrii

MELVIN: I'll ask momma,. She can handle it, She will know what to do.

GRANDMA: Okay baby, Talk to me...And I want to know all of it.

MELVIN: I take it you heard us?

GRANDMA: No now, I just know my boy. The way you walked in here is the same way you walked as a child when you're either in trouble or troubled.

MELVIN: Ahhh,. Okay.

GRANDMA: Now, I'm not exactly sure what is bothering you but, whatever it is handle it with one thing.

MELVIN: Ahh. Mmmmm

GRANDMA: And yes now I'm talking about that daughter of yours my grandbaby.

MELVIN: How do you....

GRANDMA: I'm not dead nor stupid. The buzz is in the air. My only question is what, how and when are you going to listen? I don't need to know precisely what's going on... just need to let all around me know that nothing is handled on its own.

MELVIN: Well.

GRANDMA: Exactly. Go to the well and get a drink of that good water the Lord provides. And what I mean is that you have to pray on it. NOW I know that sounds like a cliché but for real babbby. You know prayer changes things.

MELVIN: What does that mean momma?

GRANDMA: You know that the eyes can be the windows to the heart and soul? She's in trouble and it's up to you to find out why.

MELVIN: Okay

GRANDMA: In order to see the goodness of the world you have to look and seek. The way that's done is with prayer. With quantum physics there are present, past and future wrapped into our now. I can't explain it to you right now but the trust in the LORD is wrapped into this...

MELVIN: So I take it you know about Brii?

GRANDMA: I'm going to say it again; I'm not dead nor stupid. The way she interacts is nothing new. The ways of the world like that have always been around. Since the existence of mankind there have been evil spirits and good spirits. And we learn along the way how best to recognize them. But it takes the person to find that out. WE can give guidance and show them but it is their path.

MELVIN: That sound mighty passive ma.

GRANDMA: You can lead a horse to water but you can't make him drink.

MELVIN: So have you discussed Brii's interest in spells and potions with her?

GRANDMA: Yes, of course I did. But didn't need to. Judge not, that you be not judged!

MELVIN: Judge not? But your entire life has been in the bible and in the church. You of all people. How can you tolerate what amounts to satanic worship; voodoo and spells and all that crap?

Beat, disbelief

MELVIN: And why didn't you tell us?

GRANDMA: And break her trust? Son, if I break her trust,
I break her belief in me. Listen.
Melvin takes a seat on a chair adjacent to the bed:

MELVIN: All ears.

GRANDMA: The things that people do in life are for
their comfort. They are not to be faulted. Amulets and
potions and spells are an attempt at something real. Perhaps
something missing. Talk to your daughter, find out what's
missing.

MELVIN: Thanks ma.

Melvin gets up pauses, turns and leaves closing the door. It
is closed with conviction, perhaps keep the sounds of the
living room from traveling.

FELICIA: So, how did it go?

MELVIN: She never ceases to amaze me, for some reason
she already knew. She knows that Brycely is in some type
of trouble.

FELICIA: You think she knows all of it?

MELVIN: Yes.

FELICIA: With all her Bible thumping? I was sure she
would flip out!

MELVIN: Hold up now. She's is amazing. More amazing than I could even have known. I'm beginning to realize that the successes and accomplishments that we enjoy are often felt to be due to our efforts, but little do we appreciate that it's the prayers of the righteous people around up and within our lives that are primary components of our gains.

FELICIA: Oh honey, That's beautiful. The phone rings, and

rings. Felicia answers. (beat)
She sits on the sofa, hand on her forehead.

FELICIA: Hello, Yes, Yes, hospital? I am her mother, What, Where? Is she okay? Is my baby okay. OH MY GOD!! MELVIN!!! (he takes/she hands the phone to her husband)

MELVIN: Hello, yes, I am her father. What hospital? We're on our way. (hangs up the phone)

GRANDMA:(hears all the commotion, comes out of her room) What's going on out here?

MELVIN: Brii was in an accident, we're on our way to the hospital, Lets go Felicia.

End of Act 3, Scene 2

Act 3, Scene 3

It is the next day. Jenkins's front porch. There are flowers on the porch. The painting of The Praying Grandma is on an easel; COVERED, NOT SEEN BY THE AUDIENCE. Melvin is sitting on the porch, Tim enters

MELVIN: What the hell are you doing here?

TIM: Can we talk about this?

MELVIN: I'm not thinking about this right now T!

TIM: Are you really going to bring up something that happened 20 years ago ! I got past that...why would you bring it up? That's fucked up....

MELVIN: Dude, Your timing is fucked up. Why are you here? I guess its because you hear about Brii.

TIM: No, What about Brii?

MELVIN: And, where have you been?

TIM: Man, I just been trying to figure things out...

MELVIN: Well, while you've been trying to figure things out. There was an accident down on Jefferson and 3rd...Brii got hit in a cross walk So don't be coming in here with this bullshit, its not the time.

TIM: Ahhhhh Man, I didn't know, Is she okay?

MELVIN: What do you care? Apparently, your greed is more important than the life of my daughter? (stands up)I should beat your ass right now. You must be on that shit again!!?

Melvin grabs Tim in the collar. They tussle on the porch...

TIM: Look man, I'm sorry, I told you I didn't know about Brii!!

MELVIN: To hell with you man, get your sorry ass out of my yard!! And you can take this freaking painting with you, you can have the damn thing. I'm only concerned about my daughter right now.

TIM: But......

MELVIN: I said get out!!

GRANDMA: (From the living room; changing energy with intent) You two get in here, NOW!!. Why are the two of you fighting like dogs, acting like children? You know better.

(They both begin to speak at the same time)

MELVIN: You see, one day while you were in your room....

TIM: Melvin asked me to paint this picture.

GRANDMA: Wait, wait, one at a time PLEASE!! Go ahead son.

MELVIN: It was suppose to be a surprise. One day while your were in your room praying I took a picture of you. I thought it was a nice picture and thought that it would make a nice portrait, so I asked this fool….

GRANDMA: Watch it baby.

MELVIN: I asked T. if he would do the painting for me. He agreed, I gave him a deposit and now he wants to claim it as his own, and take it on TOUR thinking his sorry ass can make some money off of it.

GRANDMA: Is this true Tim?

TIM: Yes its true. But…..

GRANDMA: And he paid you?

TIM: Yes, he paid me but I tried to give him the money back.

GRANDMA: But you had an agreement, right?

TIM: Yes, but nothing in writing.

GRANDMA: And you think you can make money off it?

TIM: I really do!! Its my best work.

GRANDMA: Can I see it?

TIM: Yes you can. (Tim goes to get the picture, returns shows the picture to Grandma with revealing it to the audience)

GRANDMA: Its nice. You know, the life that we have and the appreciation of all things prior, past and future is so call represented in your works of art there...Now you know Felicia down there...

MELVIN: (interrupting) But...

GRANDMA: Breath son breath...I represent in your picture, in Tim's painting the acknowledgment of the existence of a being that is greater than all things. THIRTY PIECES OF SILVER!

Beat

We, mankind, can imagine and we can manufacture. Life given is life itself and to appreciate that is all GOD asks. That's all. Pure and simple. Now you two work this thing out, I'm tired. (Grandma goes to her room).

TIM: (to Melvin, the two continue to argue) I didn't know about Brii!

MELVIN: Why is it that you only think about yourself.
TIM: I Think about survival, cuz.

MELVIN: You'll have plenty of time to think alright.

TIM: Look, what I came here to tell you was….

MELVIN: You know what? I really don't want to hear it.

TIM: (grabs Melvin in the collar) Listen.

GRANDMA: (re-enters the room) We don't know about anything other than knowing, not believing. Believing is hope and praying is gratitude. You two look to the past to solve problems of the present, fighting over money for this painting or picture and you explain your fears in the face of uncertainty by fighting.

MELVIN: And….but what's your point?

GRANDMA: Remember the conversation we had about amulets and spells and potions?

MELVIN: Of course

GRANDMA: These are external objects in an attempt to grasp something real. When you look at it the objects are conduits to another entity. You place something on a table or a surface in order to gain entry. (beat)
But when you are alone and away from your tools, which are not at your disposal, then what do you do?

TIM: You pray?

GRANDMA; Perfect. Yes. You have your ability to reach out to the Lord; your prayers, your conversation with GOD is your conduit. It is your means of realizing your dreams. That can be where you rest; where you lay – Shambhula.

For me it's on my knees. For a dream without a plan is just a dream. NO, I don't fault Lyn for her path; I don't judge her for her efforts. Remember, life is a flow. As I have mentioned, quantum physics teach us just as the bible teaches us.

MELVIN: In what way?

GRANDMA: The present is what we have right now. The past is what we think we had. The future is what we hope may happen. Everything all at once and right now from the past to the future is what we know and what we can use. Baby, use the present for communication and the best listener is the LORD. Think about it. We cannot grab the past, we cannot feel the future and the present is a fleeting illusion. That which is present right now is not the present in a millisecond. Thus the thing we have is prayer. The one item of all three.

MELVIN: My life is the most wonderful thing you gave me and for that I am truly grateful.

GRANDMA: Well, pay attention to my prayer. It is a prayer for the ancestors and for present beings. It is a prayer for thanks and for current rewards.

FADE TO BLACK

(Lights up. Felicia arrives with Brice. There are moderate degrees of bandage material around her body.)

GRANDMA: Hey baby, how's grandma's little girl?.

MELVIN: My darling.

BRICE: Ahh....

They sit. There is a obvious moment of assurance, relief. (beat)

A familiar knock at the door breaks the moment.

They comment: "It's open Tim."

He slowly enters, sits, he is UNUSUALLY sombre . It is obvious FROM HIS SLOWED PACE

MELVIN: What do you want? (still upset with him) Why are you even here?

TIM: Remember the other day when I came by with the painting and you tried throw me out?

MELVIN: Yeah, I remember, and I am about to throw you out again.

TIM: Hold on!! The reason I came by was to tell you.

MELVIN: Look dude, like I told you, you can keep the damn painting, and while you are at it you can shove it up your....
GRANDMA: Melvin!!!

MELVIN: I'm sorry Ma.

TIM: Like I was saying, I wanted to talk to you to see if we could work something out. Then your mother started talking about the future, the present, fleeting illusions and prayers for our ancestors as well as our present beings. I got to thinking about it and I came to the realization that money is not everything. I also realized what this painting means to you. You were right, I was being selfish and had no right to try and claim that painting as solely mine. If you had not taken the picture, there would be no painting. I'm sorry man, can you forgive me? It comes from the heart as a result of your mothers prayers. Take it, its yours.

MELVIN: My brother, thank you man!! I aint gone lie though. I really wanted to choke you out. (they both laugh). Truth is, we have been through too much together to let anything come between us. I am sorry for the things I said, I......

TIM: It's cool man, lets just move on and put this behind us.

BRII: What are ya'll talking about? What portrait?

TIM: (goes and retrieves the portrait and returns. It is unveiled so that the audience can see it)

BRII: Oh wow, that's nice.

MELVIN: I call it, THE PRAYING GRANDMA!!

LIGHTS GO OUT ON EVERYTHING BUT THE PAINTING END OF PLAY

About the Author

Ken Mask, a North Carolinian native, is a testament to the versatile nature of creativity. The son of educators from Hamlet, NC, and his formative years were punctuated by exposure to the intellectual disciplines of violin and chess, which laid the foundation for his multifaceted career.

Mask is not merely a novelist, or filmmaker, but an amalgamation of these roles that defies the typical boundaries of professional identity. His early education began at the University of North Carolina, Chapel Hill, where he graduated with Honors in Philosophy and Art. The scholarly paths led him to Duke University, where he earned a Medical Degree. His journey didn't stop there but wove its way through California, New York City, New Orleans and finally, Europe.

His creative ambitions have resulted in two recent notable films. The first, "The Opera Game," traces the life of the 1850s chess grandmaster Paul Morphy. His second film, "Building

Minds with Chess," won the prestigious Programmer's Award in the Short category at the 76th Annual 2023 Cannes Film Festival. These achievements are a testament not only to Mask's storytelling prowess, but also his ability to traverse mediums with ease.

Beyond the world of film, Ken's artistic canvas extends to the realm of literature. His oeuvre spans novels, scientific papers, and children's books, showcasing a keen ability to cultivate learning and bilingual projects. Detective fiction and thrillers are his specialties, where he weaves engaging narratives that captivate readers and stimulate the mind.

His medical knowledge is not confined to the realms of Radiology, his certified specialization, but also extends to healthcare consulting. His professional pursuits provide a balance between his scientific and creative endeavors, exemplifying the unity of these seemingly disparate fields.

Simultaneously, he encourages the creative facets of his students, mentoring them in areas such as script writing, non-profit project planning, opp development, and music education. His philosophy embodies the belief that every individual has unique creative potential waiting to be unlocked. He is more than a sum of his parts. He is a symbol of creative and scientific convergence, shaping his path in the world through a love for learning, medicine, science, and art.

www.ingramcontent.com/pod-product-compliance
Lightning Source LLC
Chambersburg PA
CBHW050453110726
47899CB00003B/920